How to be an It Girl Boss:

Leveraging the Power of Relationships

Vanessa Busico

How to be an It Girl Boss

Copyright © 2016 Vanessa Busico

All rights reserved. No part of this book may be reproduced, scanned or distributed in any printed or electronic form without permission.

Cover by Moriah Grondahl/Mo Creations Design

For more info email Ladybossintl@gmail.com

For my parents, Michael and Molly, who instilled their entrepreneurship passion and ambition in me.

I love them with all of my heart.

Introduction

You have achieved an honorable and exciting position: Boss. Whether you own your business or you work in a corporate company, either way, you made it! Understandably, having such a prestigious position breeds a lot of responsibility and possibility. Yet, you are already on the path to being the It Girl Boss, through your courage and ambition to lead. I humbly salute you and your remarkable accomplishment! I would love to hear your story about how you realized your dream and became boss. I am a strong believer that behind every story, there is inspiration, even if there were a zillion challenges, tears and smiles. Hence, as the saying goes: "If it were easy, everyone would do it," and because you did it, you are an inspiration. When I think of how you made, what may have seemed impossible, possible, I think of the

French high wire walker, Philippe Petit. Monsieur Petit made the most impossible, simply possible. He walked on a high wire between the twin towers several times over. One can imagine how insane this was, yet thrilling, he conquered! Imagine the fear and the exhilaration all at once, as you watch him kneel in the middle of the high wire to bask in the experience and, of course, evade the police standing on the roof of both towers. He was the boss, he made his decisions, realized his dreams and succeeded, just like you and me. Naturally, you do not intend to walk on a tight rope or high wire, however, the sense of exhilaration and passion is often what we experience in running a business.

Being the boss and running a business is downright exciting. Everyday is an adventure, where you are making decisions, interacting with clients and employees as well as putting out fires or solving issues as they arise. Believe or not, all of these responsibilities manifest, creating the workplace environment, virtually and offline. Understandably, being in charge can be overwhelming, even emotional. I recall having experiences of women bosses when I was their employee. They were overwhelmed and authoritative, and, unfortunately, created an unhealthy work environment. These women bosses lacked the necessary skills to lead a successful and sustainable business. I recall often feeling anxious, nauseous, stressed, migraines and unhappy. I no longer desired going to work and being in such an unhealthy atmosphere. I experienced negative behaviors from my bosses, such as being harshly scolded in front of my colleagues and clients. It was not only humiliating, but also surprising to witness such behavior in these educated women, especially in the field of psychology. These instances were only motivating for me to want to change corporate culture and my life. I knew that work life could be a lot better and more enjoyable than what I experienced. I also knew that I should not have to suffer emotionally and physically for a job. Those behaviors were reminders of what not to do, as well the importance of respect and boundaries. This led me to my inspired dream of creating a business helping lady bosses to be successful in every way, including relationships in the work place.

Relationships are literally everywhere we turn; personal, professional, romantic, friendship, platonic, catatonic. You have negative types of relationships and positive types of relationships. These types exist in all environments in our world. Why is this important? Well, business survives and thrives from relationships. Relationships become the foundation, stepping stone, and crusader for business; they contribute to the success and longevity of entrepreneurship. When we talk about relationships, this refers to professional relationships, such as clients and employees. These relationship types are often taken for granted and go unappreciated. Many have forgotten that their successes are a result of the tremendous work and efforts made by the humbled staff and clients. I mention this to you because your success is as important to me as it is to you. I want to guide and teach you how to be savvy and meaningful in selecting your relationships that will help you and your business grow. Through your success, you will be able to help your clients and employees succeed in return. The process to selecting and growing your relationships is all about rapport building. The process involves several steps, however, I will cover three particular yet effective ones:

- Approach

- Communication

- Emotional Intelligence

These are some of the steps that are vital toward rapport building; they assist in producing firm, long lasting connections with clients and employees. The simplicity is what causes them to be user friendly and highly effective. Understandably, with the many complexities in this world, it is nearly questionable when something appears too simple. In this case, the simplicity of the process is just that: simple. Rapport building can be just as simple, allow me to guide you in your journey as you master the skill in building your rapport.

Chapter One

As you and I talk to one another, get to know each other, our interests, skills, accomplishments, this is a process in our rapport building. It is a genuine effort between the two of us bonding and learning. Notice that I mentioned "genuine?" If we were not genuine, the whole rapport building process would be futile. Have you experienced a conversation or an individual emitting as superficial? In other words, they seemed fake to you and probably made you feel uncomfortable, even losing interest in them. Now, this experience can exist in any type of relationship. However, I am focusing on a business relationship; a professional and platonic bond. When genuineness is involved, budding rapport building grows and excels exponentially, resulting to a long term business relationship that can lead to long term business success. If you randomly choose individuals for your business because of your urgent need to build a business or you are trying to save time, you will fail. Prospective clients and employees will sense your urgency, your superficiality, and will avoid you like the plague. Their discomfort in your presence will alarm them and motivate them to seek services or employment elsewhere. You can prevent this from happening by allowing yourself to be authentic and interested in your future clients and team. Being yourself that is positive and inviting, your style of leadership will manifest throughout your work environment and business relationships.

It is common knowledge that many different bosses have their own style of leadership. Understandably, having your own style makes you identifiable and familiar. I would be the first to tell you to be unique in your leadership abilities, but I would also tell you to lead in an encouraging and positive manner. Where am I going with this? What you exhibit in your leadership will manifest among your staff members and clients. For example, if your leadership style was authoritative, and you maintained distance from your team and clients, chances are, your business success can be short term, while your cycle of hiring and firing will run high. Healthy boundaries are good, however, maintaining distance would be perceived as cold and unwelcoming. As a result, your relationships with your team and your clients would be diving toward nonexistence, even obsolete. These individuals will not have the motivation to work hard and increase your success. You may experience clients' resistance to refer new clients to you, and may take their business elsewhere. Imagine the results if you exhibited a complete different style of leadership and how you easily grow and expand your business.

Imagine demonstrating a warm, positive and welcoming style of leadership. This time, you utilize your nurturing ability as a strength and tool when leading your team of employees (including virtual assistants, etc) and clients. As a result, your work environment and professional relationships begin to grow exponentially. You notice significant growth in your clientele, in business profits and in motivation among your team members. These people have begun to admire you and trust you. They genuinely want you to succeed as well as achieving their own success in your company. Eventually, they are comfortable in approaching you about anything business related, such as work issues or questions about a project. Their comfort stems from their confidence in your willingness to help, support, guide and lead. This makes you the It Boss.

What does an It Boss mean to you? More freedom? More stability? More responsibility? Everyone has their own perspective, myself included. However, there are tools that have aided in being a more productive and insightful It Girl Boss. Your path to being the It Girl Boss does not have to be difficult. It can be inspirational and motivating, even infectious as other lady bosses aspire to follow our example. Bear in mind: being the It Girl Boss does not include perfection. No one is perfect. I encourage you to strive to be your best and mean it. Earlier, I mentioned about utilizing your nurturing ability as a strength. As women, we have this amazing quality that is the compass in many facets of our lives, especially in rapport building. This nurturing quality gives you empathy, the ability to empathize with others. Through empathy, you can have a balance in your leadership, such as astute professionalism paired with a nurturing stance toward your team. In other words, you can exhibit a strict demeanor when delegating directions as well as provide a compassionate side to those in need of extra support. Allow me to emphasize that it is completely acceptable to be compassionate. This is not a sign of weakness! I strongly urge you to not compare yourself to the male competitors in leadership; their style and their perspectives are completely different than yours.

In fact, compassion and nurture make women better leaders! Nurturing leaders are able to assist where emotions are involved, able to reach deeper levels and achieve effective solutions.

Chapter Two

Nurturing leaders have a greater ability to handle work place issues. If you still find yourself struggling in this area, do not be hard on yourself. Handling issues and emotional employees or clients can be challenging. Yet, it is not difficult to learn how to manage and resolve in a short but effective manner. Once you develop the skills, you will find how much easier it will be to solve issues in less time. As time progresses, you will witness employees and clients draw closer to you, while instilling more trust in you. The next thing you know: you are becoming the It Boss. It is my job to teach you the methods in strengthening your qualities, developing mediation skills and delegating through ease.

Being the It Girl Boss can be a no brainer or extremely difficult, depends on how your perceive it. Either way, you should not have to struggle or second guess yourself. Through strengthening your qualities, I encourage you to take the time and think about what your qualities may be. They can include confidence, efficiency, dependability, etc. The idea is that you realize your uniqueness, which will draw others closer to you, even inspire them. Your uniqueness is also a strength of yours; being you that no one can mimic. It is not enough nor effective to be like everyone else and blend. No darling, it your time to shine in the most memorable and infectious way! Why not channel your uniqueness? Simply radiate from inside out along with few added skills.

If you have been in a leadership position for quite some time, I applaud you for this milestone. Even though you have a wealth of experience leading, it is okay to learn new skills or to seek support. It is a positive approach to ask for help. This can arrive at the perfect time, because leading can sometimes be lonely and overwhelming. What new skills can you add to your repertoire? Perhaps, your mission to expand your business or sustain working relationships can use a bit of guidance or a makeover. There are five steps that I use in building productive and sustainable rapport. They provide a foundation and actionable steps to apply immediately. This will help in developing and maintaining long term relationships for the sake of your business success. I will share a few usable steps with you. The most imperative step is the first step: the Approach. Approach refers to how you address yourself to someone, and how to connect with the individual. When you think about your approach to clients and staff, or their approach to you, how is it usually conducted? There are different styles of approach, depending on the person, custom and culture. For example, in Asia business approaches would consist of a meeting in an intimate setting, like lunch or dinner, engaging in a conversation about family, historical upbringing, etc. The purpose is to get to know one another, identifying strengths and weaknesses through verbal exchange. Europe practices similar styles, time is not rushed, and often a meal or drinks are included. Your approach will determine how others respond to you; the result of their response will make or break your business relationships. While retaining your unique qualities, your approach should also be engaging, responsive to conversations, having open body language and using a welcoming tone of voice. Now, you do not have to hold their hand and sing to them. Yet, it will benefit in having the individual feel comfortable in your presence. A guarded, distant approach will only increase discomfort and awkwardness, which can drive away anyone. If your struggle is presenting an engaging approach, then practice actionable steps to remedy this issue. One actionable step that I find helpful is to partner with someone you know well, and are comfortable to be with. Think of a scenario where you are speaking with a staff member or a client.

Utilize the scenario you chose and practice an engaging dialogue with your partner. The difference will be in using a more open approach then you would normally exhibit. Techniques in an open, engaging approach includes a firm, yet warm handshake, smile, and give eye contact. Also, show genuine interest in the conversation, use consideration when sharing your reason or interest in meeting them. Ask them how they are doing, how their family is doing, and compliment them on their accomplishments. Do not forget to share something about yourself. It helps the individual to have a better understanding of who you are and where you are coming from. This even provides them with more ease about being in your presence. When the meeting is coming to a close, be the first to thank them for taking the time to meet with you and extend your hand for a handshake. Be sure to maintain eye contact and a genuine smile, to ensure a positive approach. At the end of the scenario practice, ask your partner to share their perspective and opinion on your approach. Ask them to provide you with constructive criticism; this is not a time to tear you down and make you feel bad. Their feedback will help you be to be more aware of where to make improvements and what skills to strengthen. Most importantly, your approach will no longer be a struggle for you, after all, practice makes familiarity. This technique is meant to be simple and uncomplicated. You would be surprised at how many business leaders are willing to skip the whole handshake and eye contact, which can pave the road to disaster. Of course you are not trying to become BFFs with the person, but you do want to help them feel more comfortable, especially if they are bringing business projects to you. Another step that is just as important and goes hand in hand with approach is communication, which will be discussed in the next chapter.

Chapter Three

Communication and approach compliment one another and exude a more natural feel when you put them into practice. Communication that is open and clear makes a world of a difference! This means having conversations without interrupting or rushing one another. Communication is the perfect tool to allow yourself, others and myself to express thoughts, feelings and requests. Now, it does not all have to be emotional, but it does require some emotion, respect and alternating turns to speak. So, if you find yourself talking over your team or clients, even interrupting at times, now is the time to practice a different style. Often times, poor communication skills create issues and break down rapport; it can certainly hurt your business. To avoid these potential issues, I utilize a simplified technique that is easy to remember and highly effective. You may already be familiar with using "I" statements, such as "I feel," "I think," "I hear." If you are familiar with them, you may have forgotten how simple and how effective they are. They can really elicit profound results by going into deeper levels of verbal exchange without the psychobabble. Using the "I" statements will bring clarity and strengthen the bond between you and your team. You will achieve a level of understanding in concise conversations. In fact, another tool known as Reframing, brings forth the validation and positive verbal exchange needed in effective rapport building. Everyone deserves to feel validated and understood in a positive way. Reframing helps individuals like you and me feel heard and understood without negativity. Reframing is a method in repeating what was told to you in a different way, but using a more positive alternative. When you use Reframing and "I" statements, it will help the other individual feel validated that you are listening and engaged with them. You will feel more confident and comfortable as you connect well with the person. You can see how words and behaviors can have a positive or negative effect on anyone, including yourself. Imagine the effect that emotional intelligence would have on these behaviors and thought processes. Next, we will explore another step involving emotional intelligence.

Chapter Four

When you can identify the difference between positive and negative emotions, you are using your emotional intelligence, another technique that you may or may not be aware of. Emotional intelligence is so useful in a lot of situations, especially in rapport building. Have you noticed your emotions interfering with rapport building? Or, are you able to separate your emotions when working with people and high tense situations? What you bring to your environment will set the tone on mood and behavior of anyone present. Understandably, talking about emotions or emotional subjects can be sensitive for you or those you know. However, it is okay to feel sensitive about certain subjects, experiences, but it is not okay if you allow your emotions, especially negative ones, to control your thoughts, your decisions and your behavior. The good news is: you have the ability to set the tone you want for your business team and your environment. Since emotions can sometimes be messy, there is a way to keep things clear and simple. One method is awareness; being aware of your own feelings and what you exhibit as an example to your team and your clients. Since you are the leader, people will follow what you do. As part of awareness, you have to keep in mind that no one is a mind reader. In other words, if you are upset or disappointed about something, no one will know what upsets you until you tell them. If there is a personal issue from home upsetting you, it is always best to leave the issue at home and not bring it to work or place of business. Separating your emotions is a method that takes practice to implement, and can be very effective as you lead the way as an It Girl Boss.

    Learning how to separate your emotions does not have to be time consuming, nor does it need to be painful. The idea is to know that there is a time and place for everything. Would you have your coffee and bagel during your presentation to prospective clients? Of course not, you would wait until your break time or private time. It is the same idea in regards to your feelings and emotions. You can mediate your feelings by asking yourself: "what is the priority?" "What needs to be solved first?" When asking yourself these questions, you are focusing your thoughts to work toward achieving a productive solution. You may not notice immediately, but your feelings will be calmer and resonate more positivity, while your thoughts target on specifics to produce results. Hence, you will find yourself completing tasks without wasting any energy or time. Your team of employees and clients will become influenced by your example, because the end goal is to obtain a tangible outcome. The next thing you know, you and your team form a stronger, more respectful bond. You just became an It Girl Boss right before their eyes.

Being the It Girl Boss is completely achievable, tangible and deserving! No special powers are needed, only added or polished skills. Remember, you are human and it is perfectly fine to falter every once in a while. You learn and become your best from your mistakes, just as I do. Those mistakes make you stronger, sharper and more prepared. Being the It Girl Boss also means that you can take the time to enjoy your coffee and bagel. In fact, influence your team to take the needed breaks to recharge their energy. Enjoy your status, because you earned your way through hard work, determination and persistence to be your own boss, or the It Girl Boss. This also places you in a special position: creating positive change in corporate culture and entrepreneurial industry. We are the new pioneers breaking ground and building evergreen success. I would not be here today as my own boss if I did not believe it was possible to instill change, deepen rapport, while forming success at once. Well, lovely It Boss, take that beautiful thing called responsibility and obtain extraordinary results through one simple tactic: bridging the gap.

Epilogue

As you can see it is quite tangible to reach the level of an It Boss. Utilizing simple, yet effective actionable steps to build a foundation not only for your business but a successful one, begins with rapport. Approach, Communication and Emotional Intelligence are just the initial stages of rapport building as well as business growth followed by many more tools for ongoing success. However, the three tools I shared are the key formations that ensure connections on a trustworthy level that will guide in the selection of your clients and team members, as well as sustain current business relationships for the long term. There is always room for growth and improvement; it is never too late to learn. Below you will find actionable steps that you can practice immediately and apply them to your business. These will embark your leadership journey are your position yourself as the It Boss. If you found the exercises to be helpful and would like to learn more, contact me. We can create an action plan that reflects your needs and goals to be the It Boss that you envision yourself to be. The goal is to give you the opportunity to enhance your rapport with current clients and team members, by utilizing your action plan, which can also serve as a guide for future business rapport. Remember: long term rapport equals long term business and long term success. By all means, share your responses, I would love to hear your answers and get to know you. You can email me at Ladybossintl@gmail.com. Let's begin:

What kind of leadership do you envision yourself presenting? How would you approach your team and clients to achieve the leadership that you envision?

What type of communicator are you? What changes would you make in your communication style?

What is your comfort level (10 being best) in handling workplace issues? How would you handle your personal emotions?

What leadership style do you currently practice? What would you like to change?

How do you feel about incorporating your nurturing abilities with leadership?

What does rapport mean to you? How would you approach rapport building?

Rapport that you have developed previously, were they short term or long term and why? Which would you prefer for future business?

What type of environment do you want to create for your work environment or place of business? What steps are you willing to take to achieve that type of environment?

In your own words, what does it mean to be an It Girl Boss? What steps would you take to become the It Girl Boss?

www.ingramcontent.com/pod-product-compliance
Lightning Source LLC
Chambersburg PA
CBHW070425190526
45169CB00003B/1412